The Birdhouse

The Birdhouse

Tim Peeler and
Clayton Joe Young

Redhawk
Publications
2020

For all the women who fight their way through,
and also, for all those who can't.

Tim Peeler, April 2020

Published by

Redhawk Publications
2550 US Hwy 70 SE
Hickory NC 28602

ISBN: 978-1-952485-03-9

To purchase framed prints or purchase books for resale
please email rcanipe@cvcc.edu

Books by Tim Peeler and Clayton Joe Young

West of Mercy

We See What We Want to See with Kelly Carroll

Books by Tim Peeler

Knuckle Bear

L2 a Poetry Novel

Rough Beast

Wild in the Strikezone: Baseball Poems

The Easter Monday Baseball Game

Henry River: an American Ruin - Poems

Checking Out - Motel Poems

Waiting for Godot's First Pitch: More Poems from Baseball

Touching All the Bases: Poems from Baseball

Outlaw Ballplayers with Hank Utley

Baseball in Catawba County with Brian McLawhorn

Curt Flood and other Baseball Poems

Blood River: Selected Poems 1983-2005

Fresh Horses

Waiting for Charlie Brown with Ted Pope

Writers on the Storm with Carter Monroe and Robert Canipe

Books By Clayton Joe Young

Food Cultures Recipe Cookbook- Henry River Mill Village (photo editor and contributor)

Newton: Then and Now (photo editor and contributor)

The Last of the Young Men

A Celebration of Heritage

Mountain Folk

Country Roads with Poet Scott Owens

Keeping Our Traditions

North Carolina: Places and Things

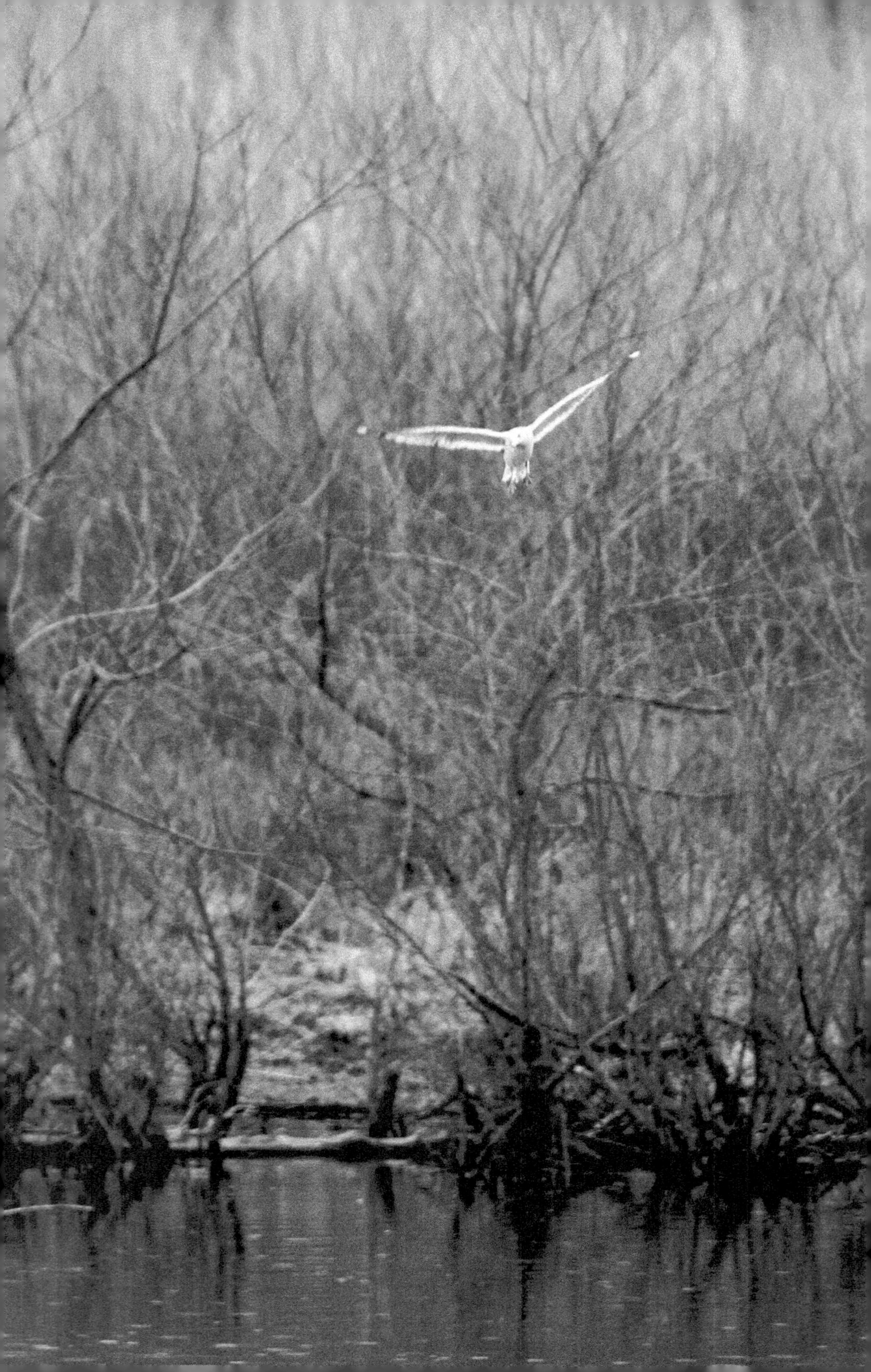

"A Robin Redbreast in a Cage
Puts all Heaven in a Rage."

William Blake "Auguries of Innocence"

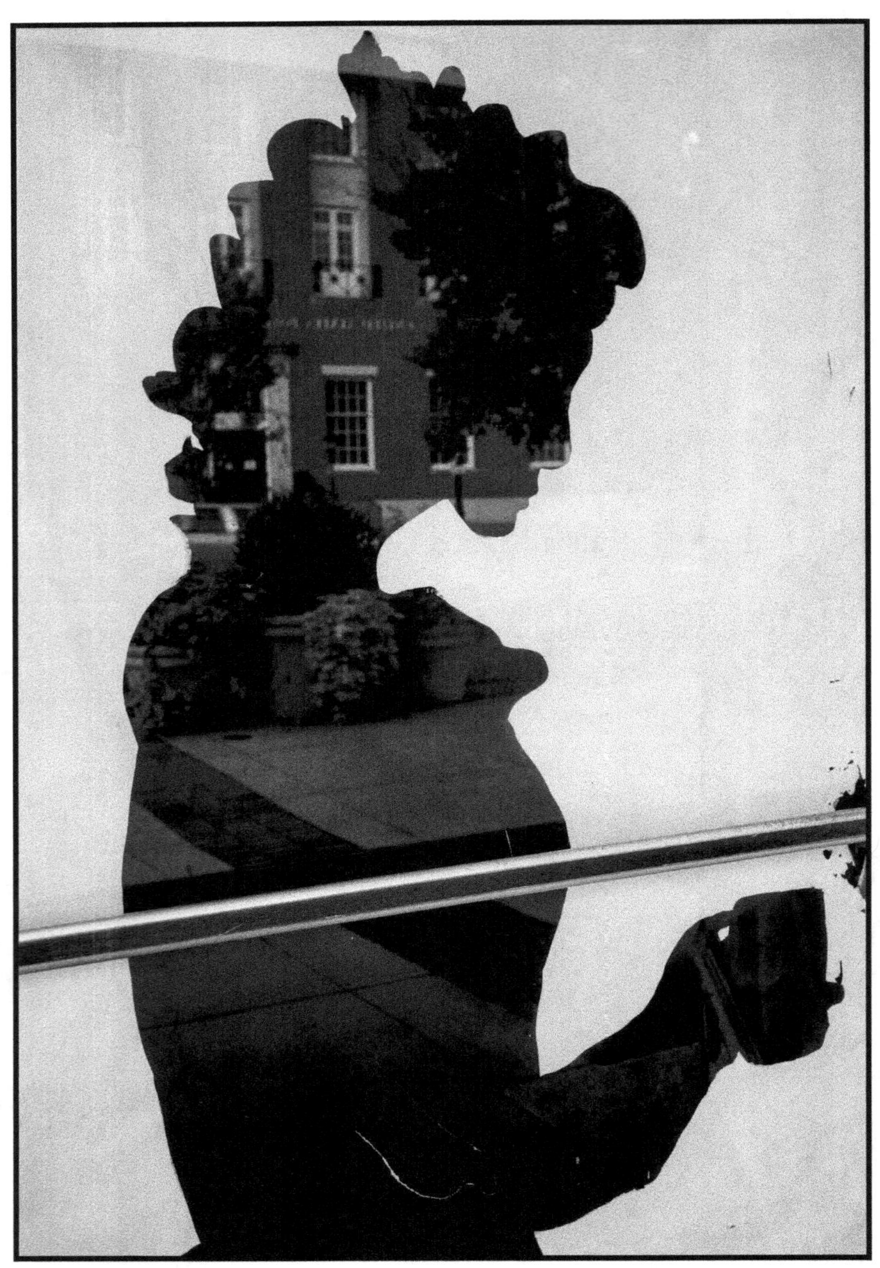

I was watching Claude mow the backyard
Out the picture window in the sunroom,
Scrolling through facebook on my laptop
Putting off the homework I needed to do
For that biology class I gotta take for the program
When I noticed something funny going on
And sat straight up to get a better look.

Claude likes to mow up and down
Up and down, same way he does
Other stuff if you know what I mean,
Never in slow squirreling circles,
Just lines, lines, and lines, he says
It makes the yard bristle evenly.

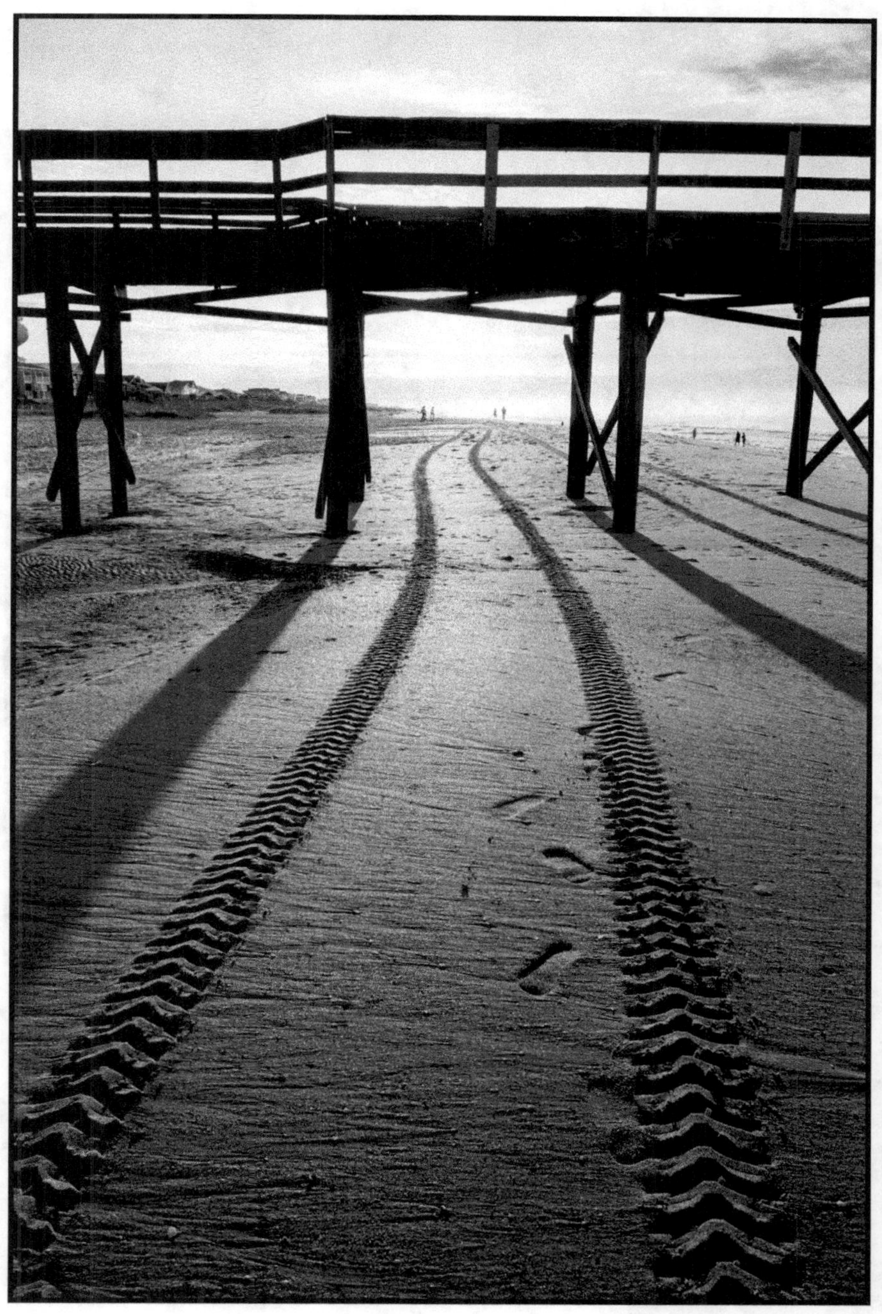

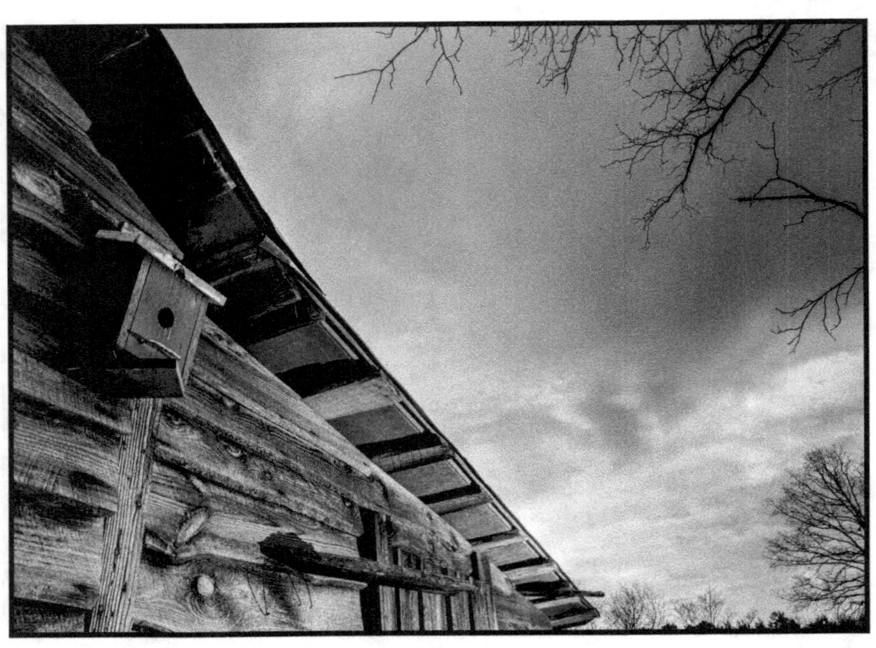

And that's what he was doing, each line
Drawing closer to that row of dogwoods
He planted the year we both got married
To each other, and in that middle dogwood,
The one that bloomed pink each spring,
He had hung the birdhouse that no good
Harley Lawson, once my boyfriend, made
For me, with its cockeyed roof and
Its oversized hole, like some warning to me
Of just how bad things might have been;
In my community college English class,
Besides how to use a semicolon, I also
Learned that this is a symbolic action.

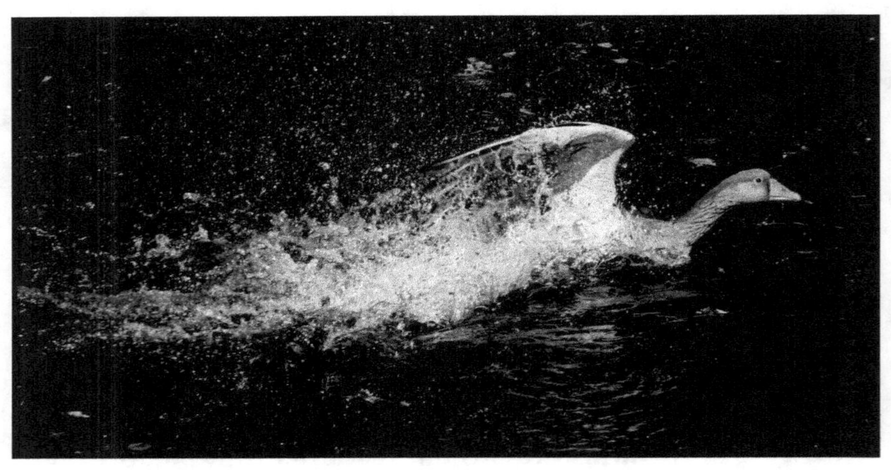

Claude started right behind the house,
Edging as close as he could to my flowers,
Knowing all the hours I stooped and crawled
Amongst them every April, daring me to
Say something; my psychology instructor
Called this passive-aggressive behavior,
Same as how he used to ease up on me
In the bed nights I said I didn't want to.

Back and forth, back and forth,
Claude maneuvered that John Deere
Mower he'd bought five years ago
Just after he lost his job and he knew
There was no way in hell we could
Afford it; he'd made five or six trips
Past the window when I noticed the snake head
Poke out from the bird house hole.

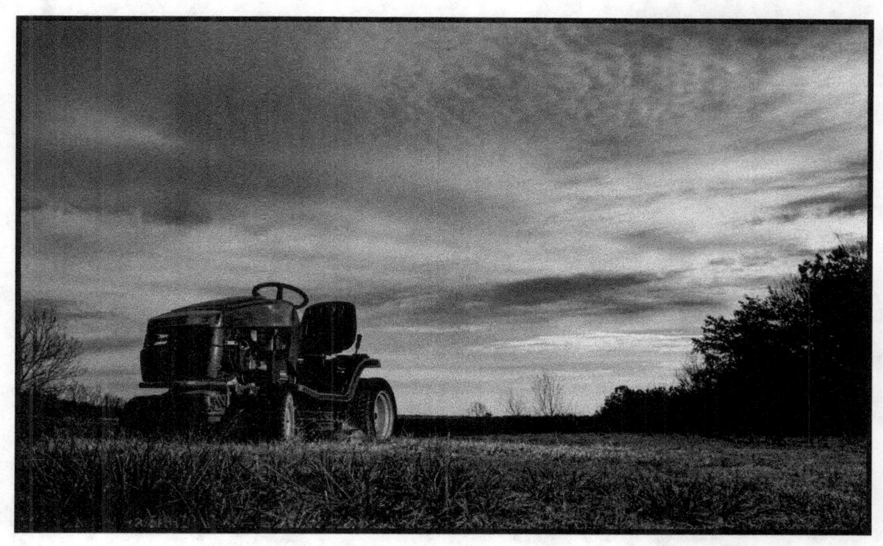

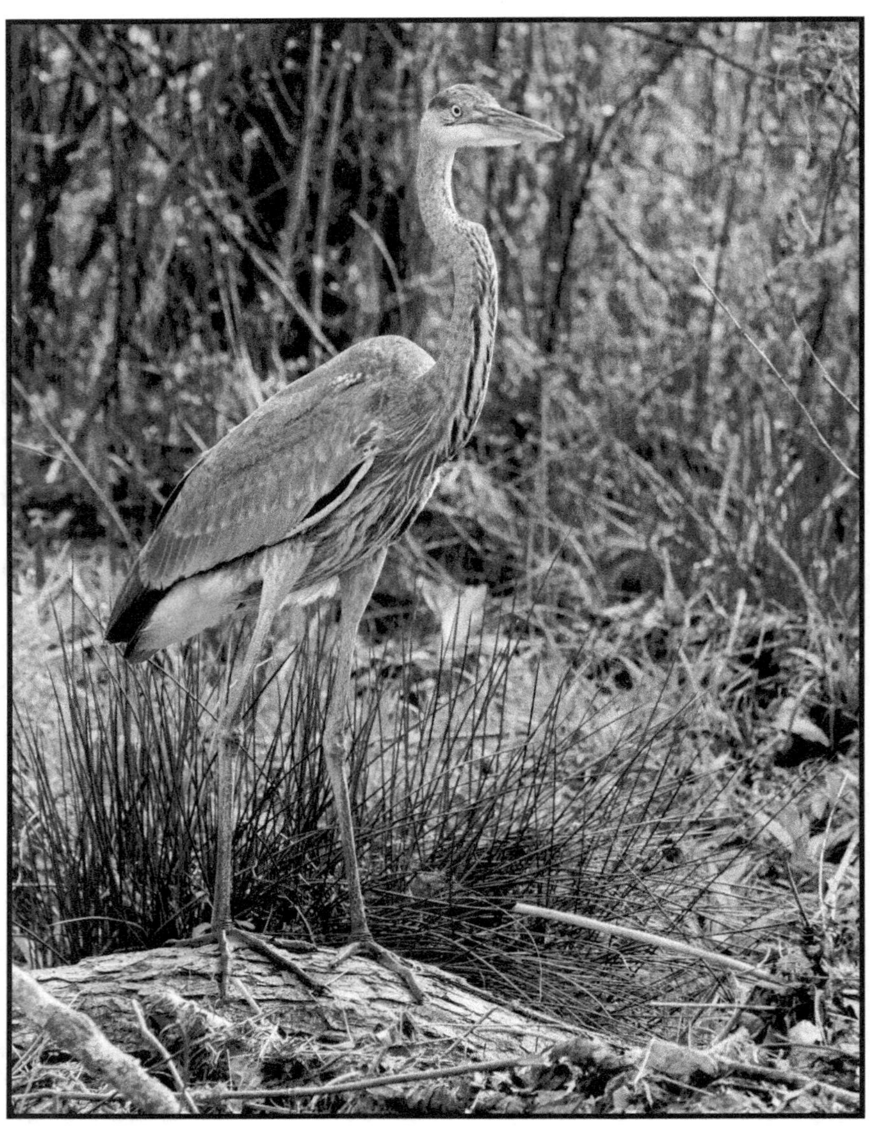

This was one of those many times
I wished my Momma was still alive;
She was part of the last generation
That knew all the plant names
In the wild, what any animal might do;
However, Google is the next best thing
To my dead Momma, and I typed the question
Fast like all the young kids did, slapping
The keys arbitrarily, a word I'd learned
In Developmental Reading last year.

Will a copperhead climb a tree? I asked
The great wizard of the Internet, and
In a blink the wizard unleashed what they
Told me in computering are called spiders,
And the first hit they sent back was from
Snake removal.com who said copperheads
Will sometimes climb trees when cicadas
Are in season or even to sun themselves.

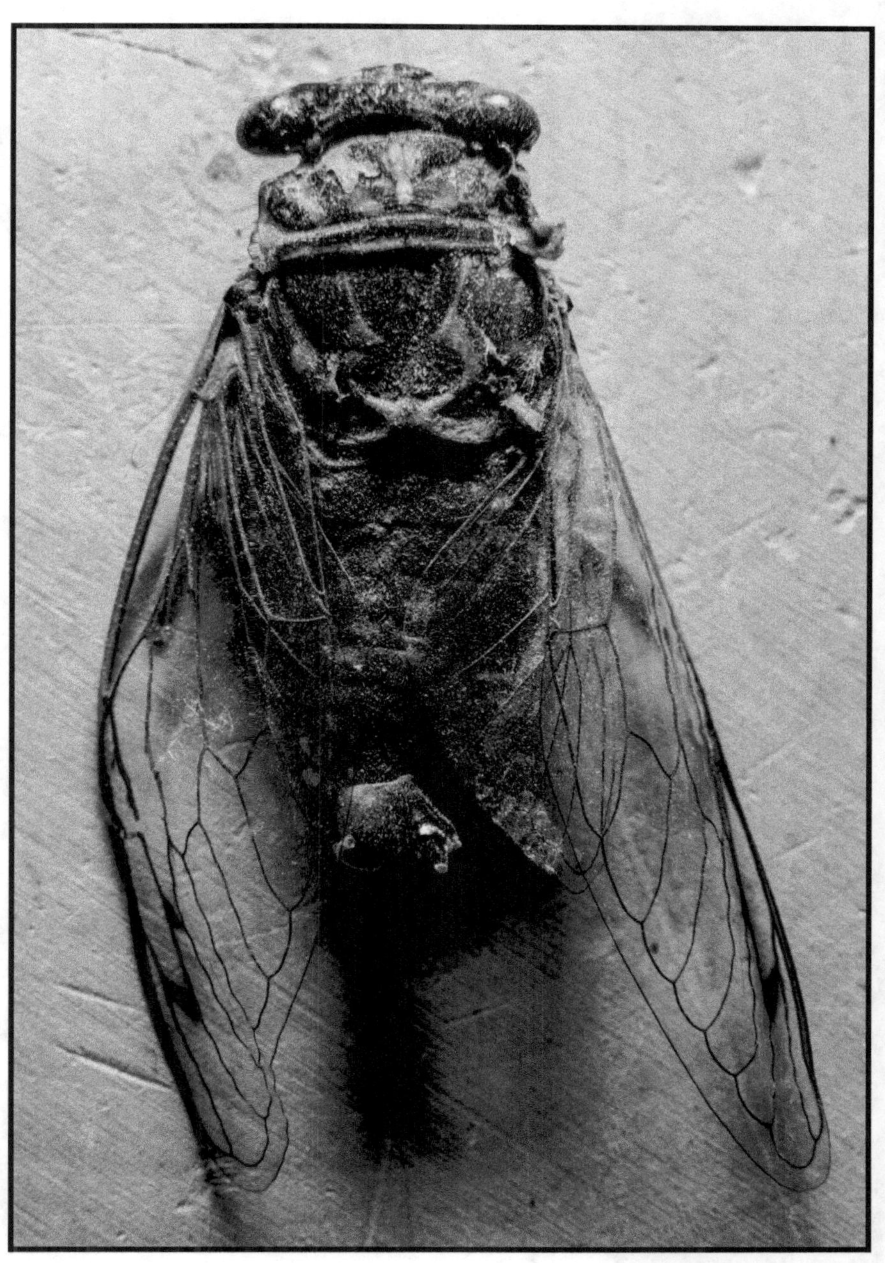

Farther down the page, notice I said
Farther where before I went back
To school I would have said further,
But now I know that further means
Psychological distance, anyway
It said the copperhead's venom
Is the least toxic of all the pit vipers;
Then there was a picture of one,
So realistic that it almost paralyzed me
With fear just to look at it.

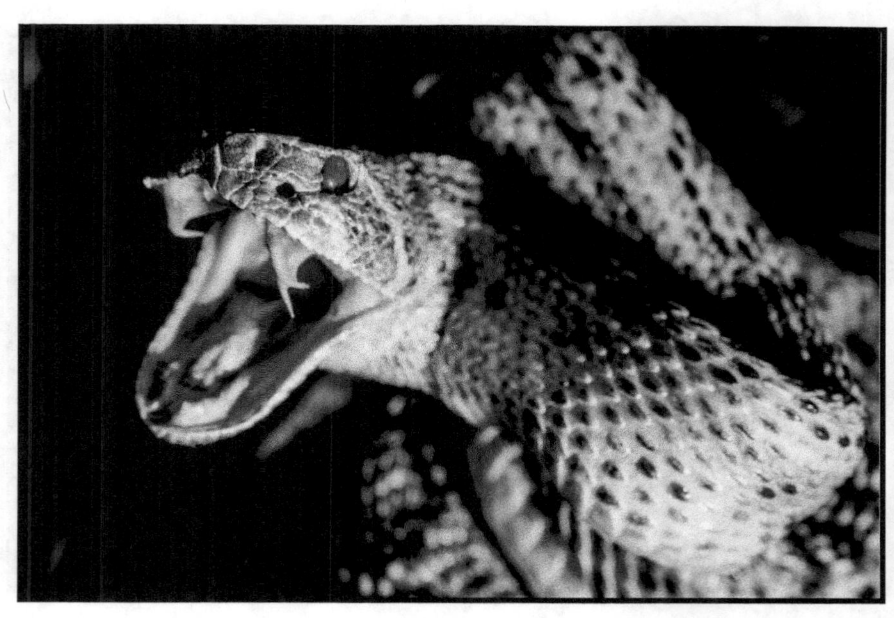

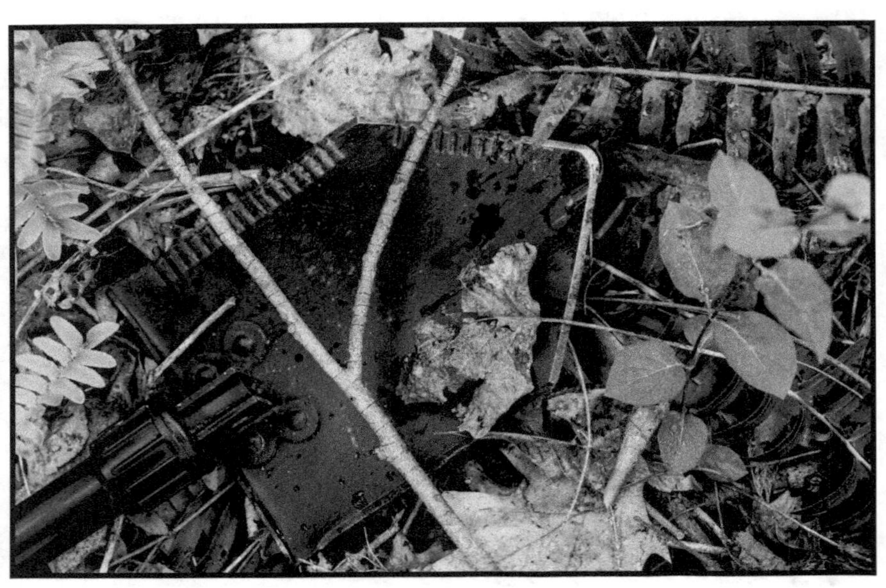

Suddenly I remembered Claude
And looked up to see that he was
Nearly halfway across the yard,
And that each time he passed,
That little shovel shaped head
Came a little farther out the house,
Again meaning physical distance.

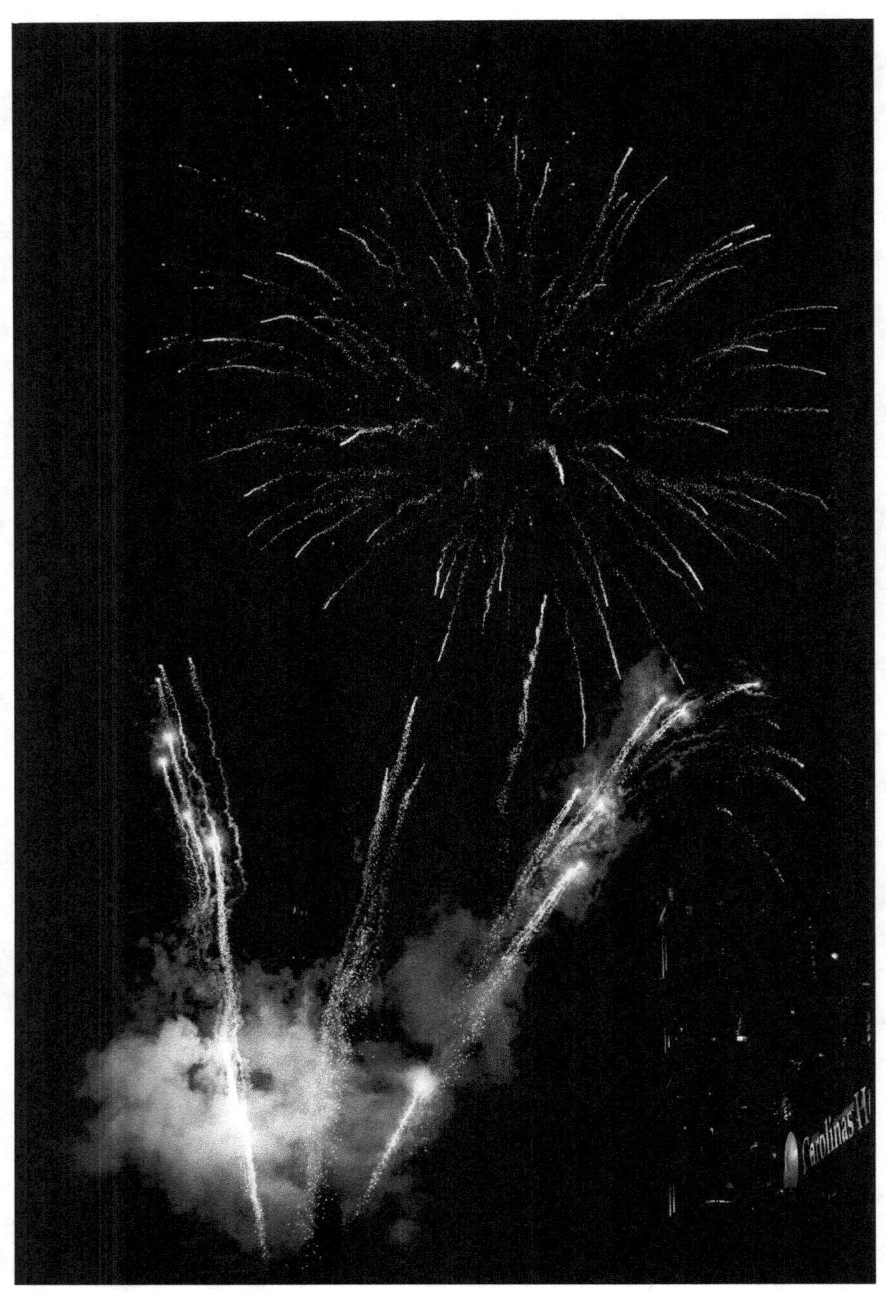
Carolinas

It’s difficult to believe I still remember,
But that first time we did it,
We had just got back from a church
Softball game where he hit a
Home run to win it, and he the
Youngest player on the team.
There was no one home; his parents
And little brother were at an auction.

We stood for a moment
Inside his bedroom door;
We kissed hard and deep
And when I opened my eyes
I could see his life size poster
Of Cal Ripken Jr. set to field
The ball in his Orioles uniform.

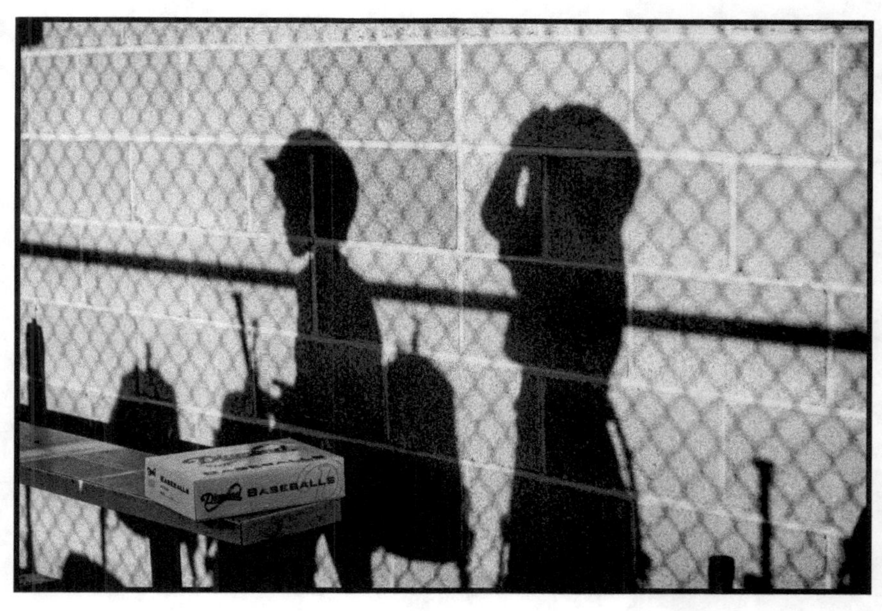
BASEBALLS

He shut the door and pushed me
Back a few feet; then something
Happened: I heard his voice
In a way I'd never heard it before;
Take your top off, he said, but
It was like a teacher or the principal
Telling me to get to class;
It was the voice of authority.

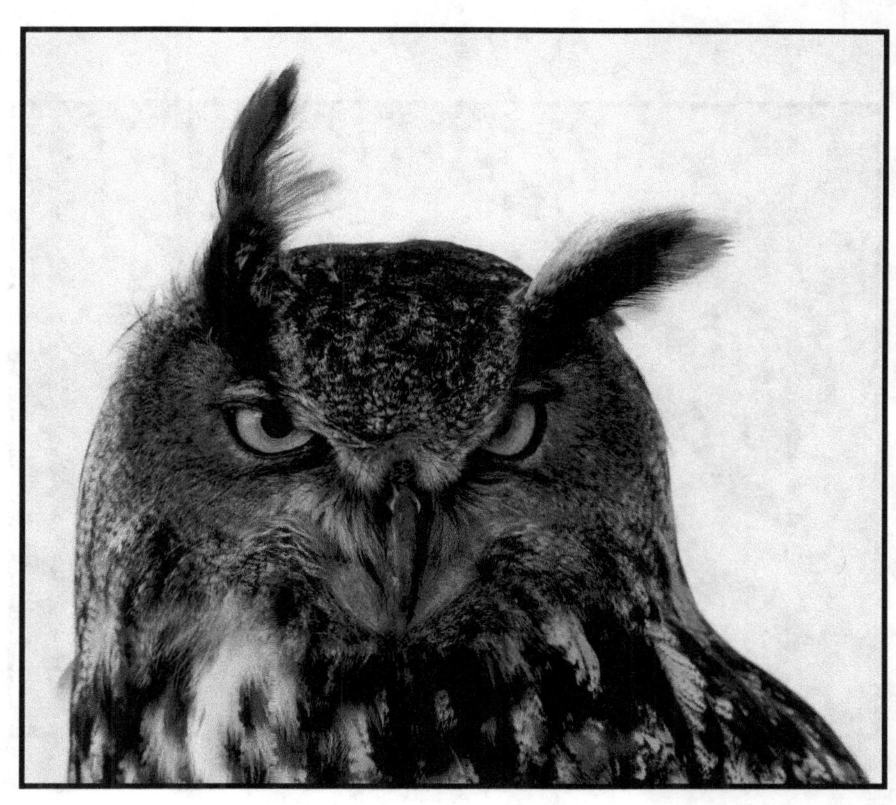

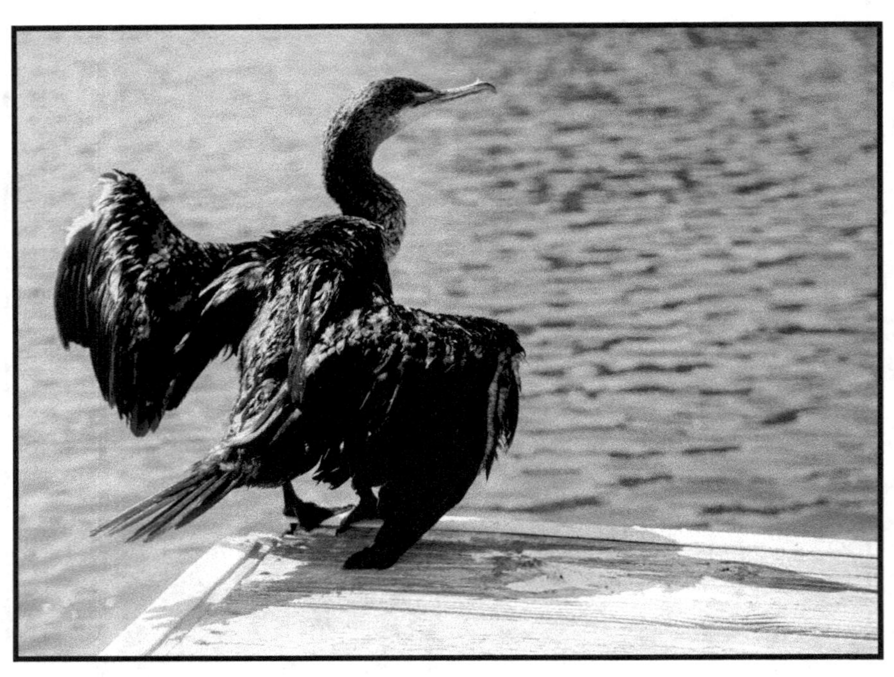

I wasn't sure I was ready,
But I could not disobey;
According to my psychology book,
I'd been conditioned to listen and comply,
But I have to admit that I wanted
Him to see my breasts shake free,
And I'd practiced some of those
Poses I'd seen the women do
In the magazines Daddy
Stashed under his recliner.

Now he tells me what to do
Like I'm a dog, the cook, or a maid,
In a voice so dull, so vacant
Of emotion, that it makes me
Want to stick him with one
Of the needles we practice with
In the program
To see if he still bleeds.

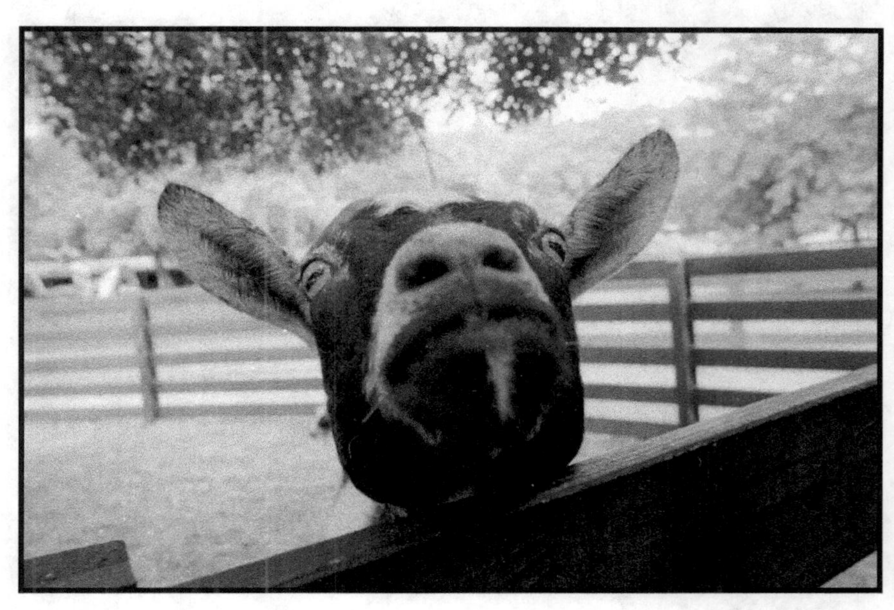

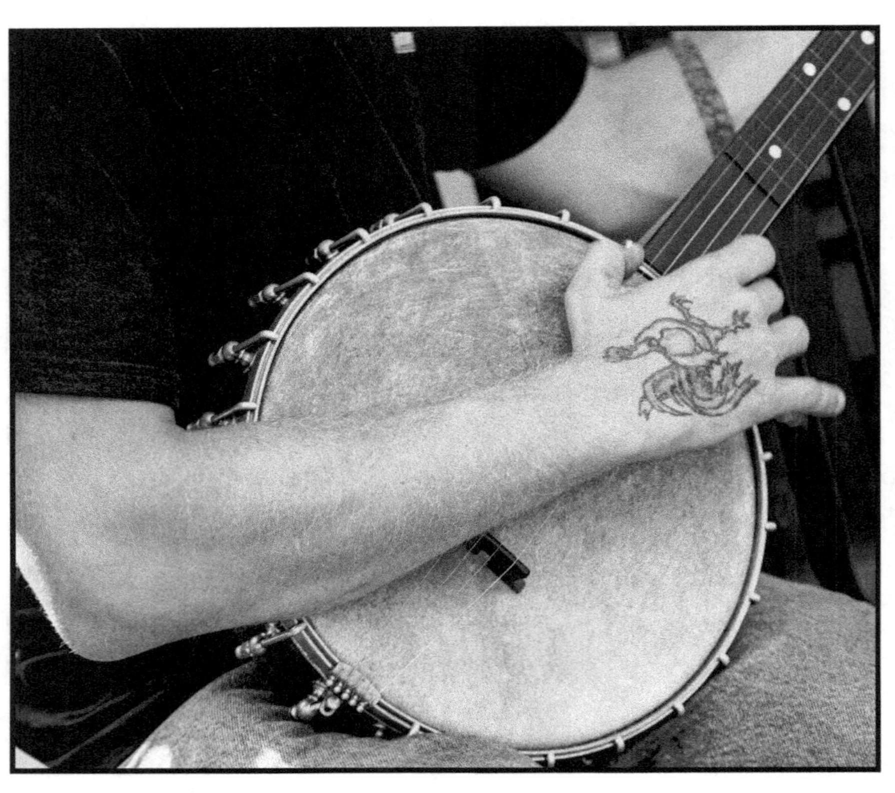

Rarely does the victim die,
The article continues, because
With a human, it is only a warning
And the snake will not hang on
Long enough to inject a lethal amount.
Claude has on his IPOD turned up
Playing that bro country shit
That drives me completely crazy
And wearing his Jimmie Johnson
Lowe's ball cap turned backwards
Like a ninth grade punk.

Claude Jr. refuses to communicate
Except by text message, and his
Daddy refuses to text message,
So not only does Jr. never come over,
But they almost never talk;
Same for our daughter Misty
Who's disappeared with her boyfriend
That she told me reminded her
So much of her father
In a trailer on Casar Mountain.
We all suspect that they are heavily
Into holy roller religion, drugs or both.

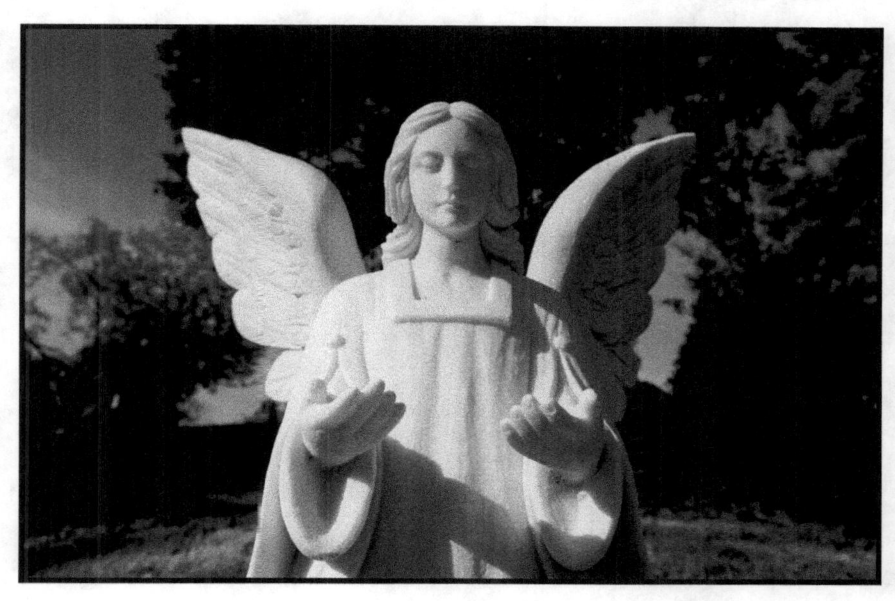

Well, this is just hard to believe,
But the website says the main
Strategy a copperhead employs
In order to avoid conflict
Is to remain completely still;
I guess this little devil
Failed to get the memo
Because I can see him arching
His neck moving his head
A little bit from side to side
As if his whole body
Is coiled up beneath him.

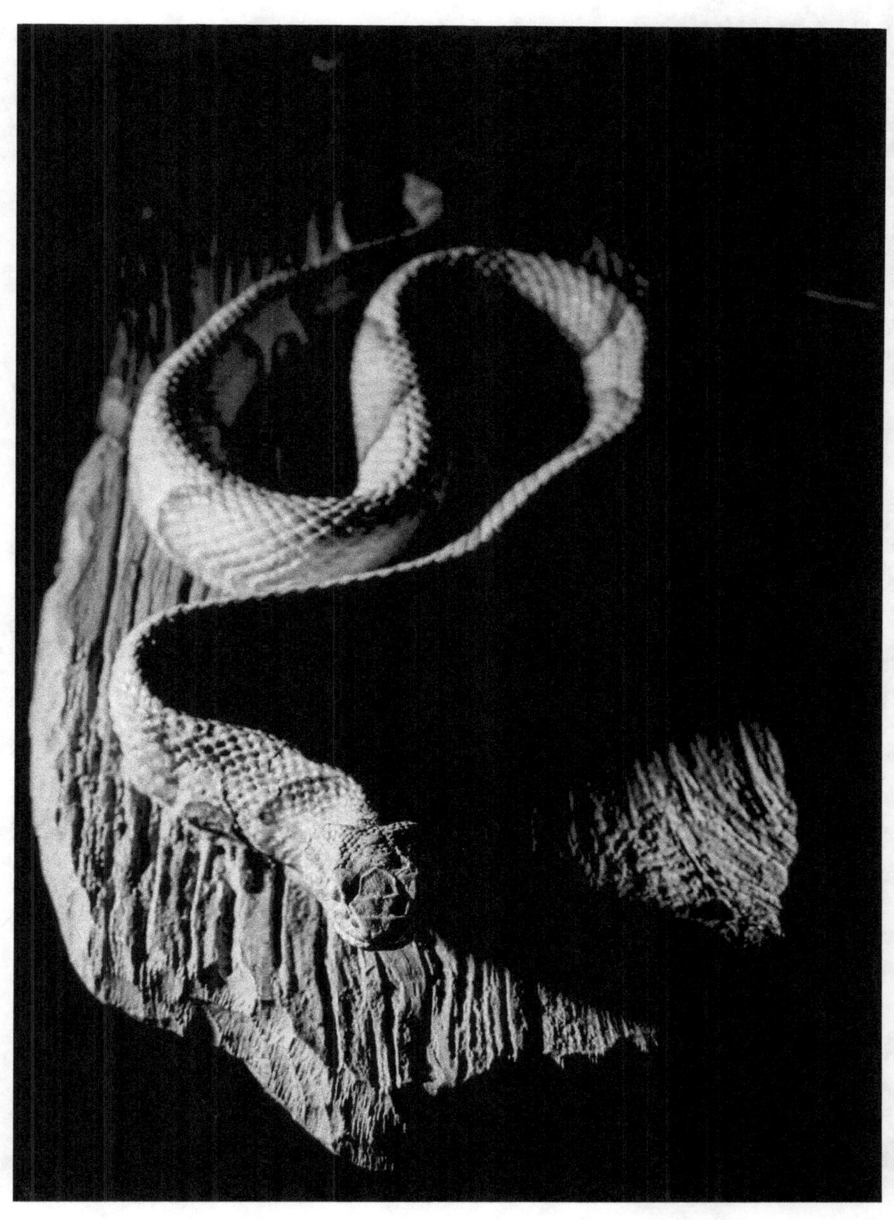

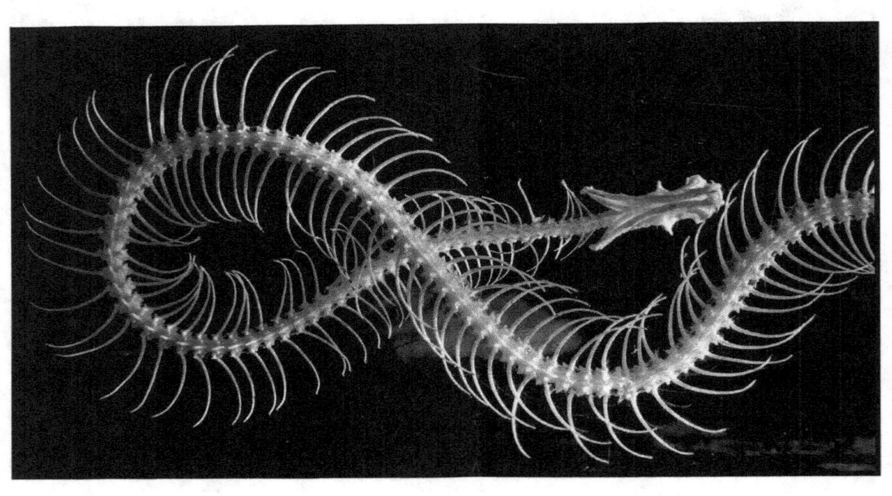

Eventually, I'm going to have to
Go out there and warn old Claude;
I'm not the kind of person
Who would let her husband
Get bit by a venomous snake—
I learned in biology class the other day
Not to call them poisonous—
I am not that kind of person
Even after what he did
To me the other night.

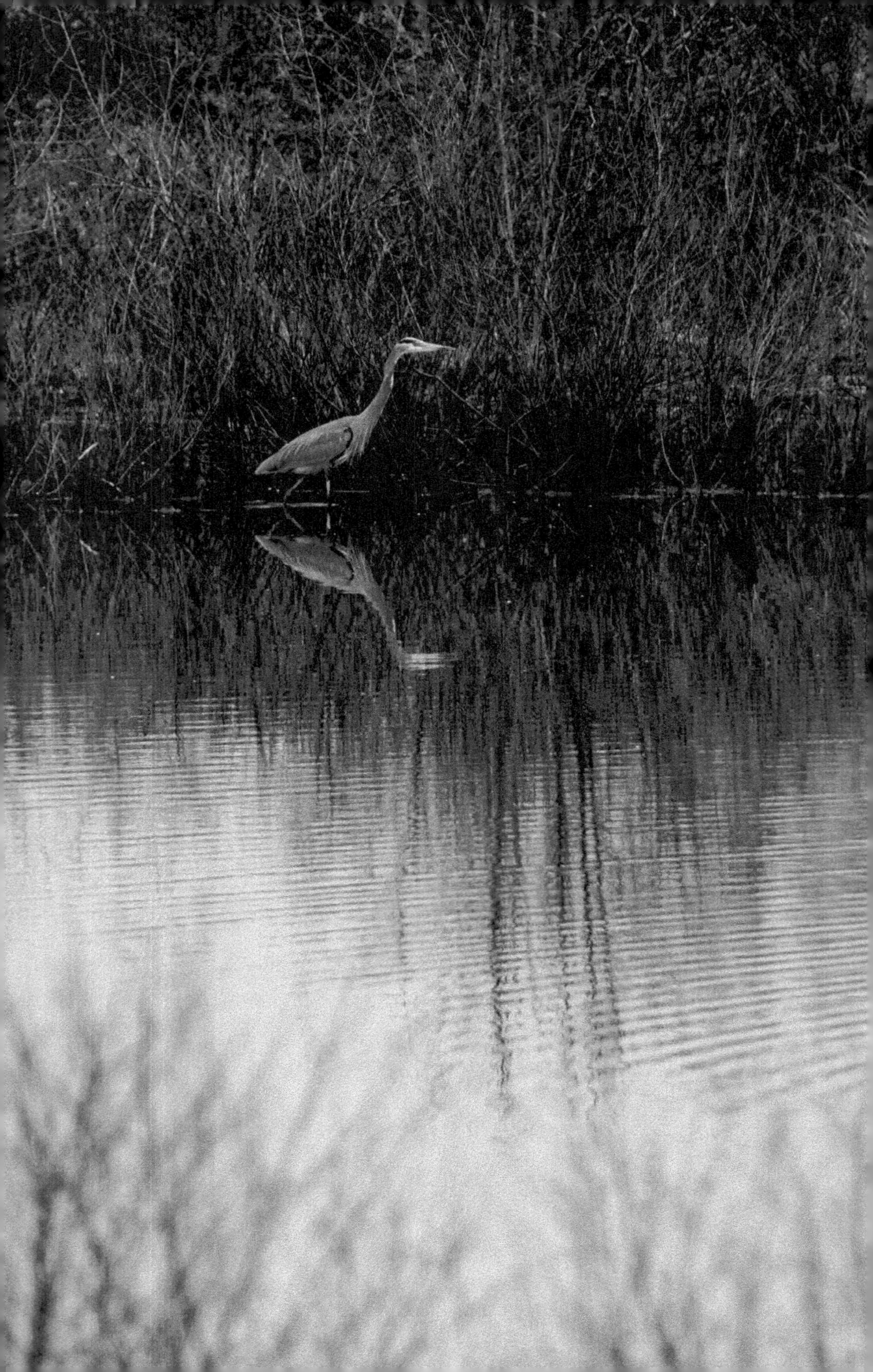

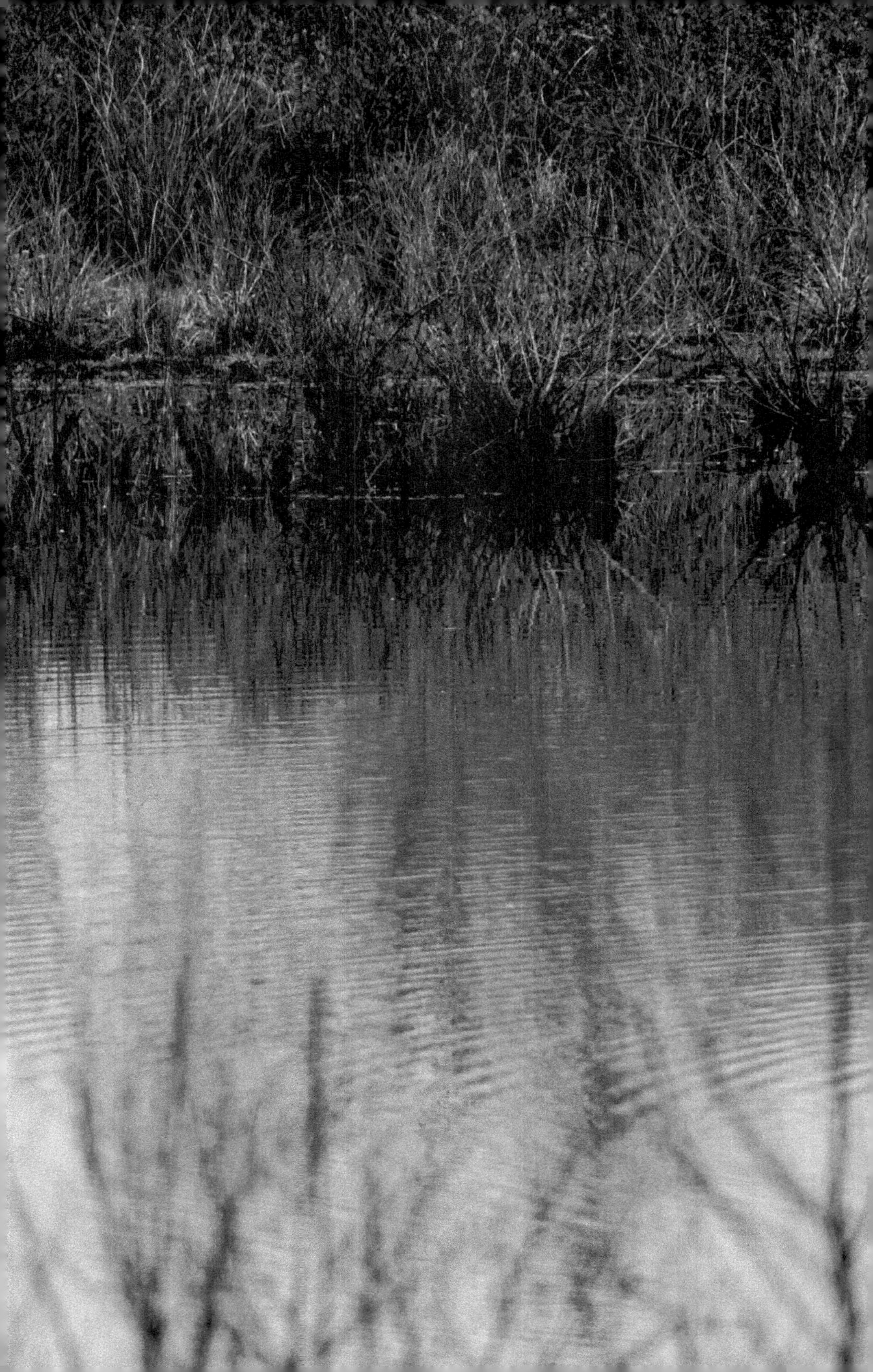

I was sitting right here
In the sun room
Just like I am now
With a couple textbooks
Laid out on the table
Checking my facebook
To see which of my friends
Might be posting twenty year-old
Pictures of themselves
In order to have a whole group
Of people click on that like button
And leave little comments
Like "beautiful," or "so hot,"
Or Dah-h-h-h-h-m yore
Three syllable gorgeous.

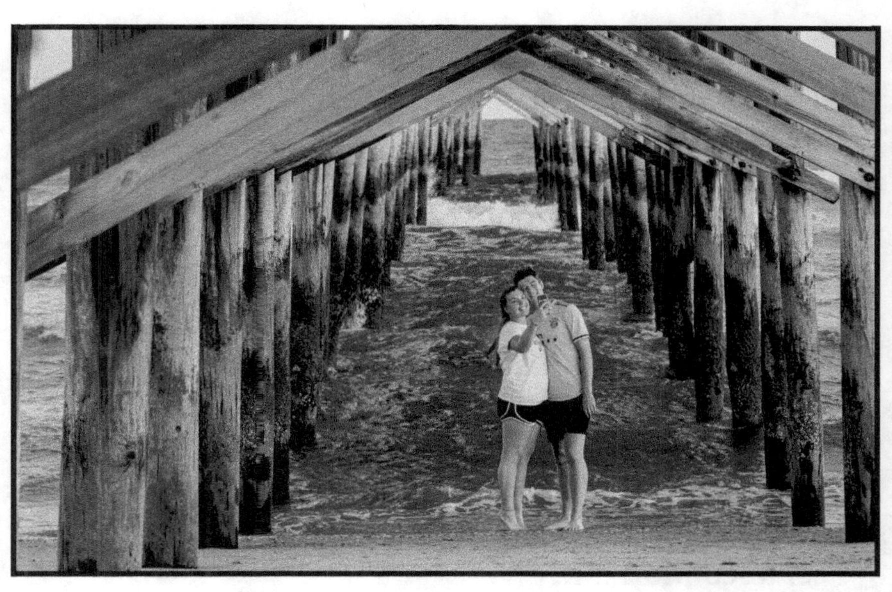

I didn't hear him come up
And he caught me scrolling
Slowly across a half naked
Picture of some male dancers
That one of the girls
From my program had posted.
Claude wants me to make money,
But he hates the program
And me learning new stuff
And especially me meeting
Smart people that make
His dumb truck driving ass
Feel uncomfortable.

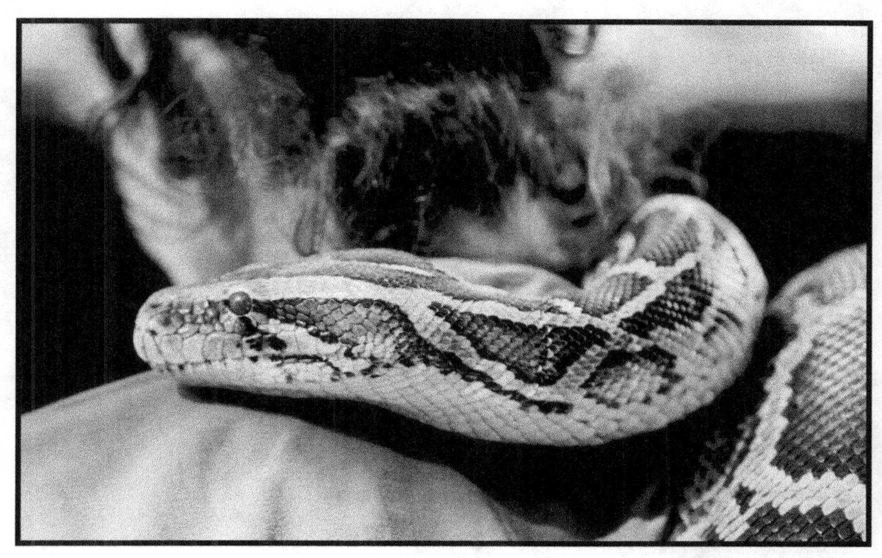

The first thing I felt were his hands,
And when I say it was not in a good way,
I am attempting to make light of the horror;
He squeezed my throat so hard
That my windpipe was shut, and
He held me that vicious way
For fifteen or twenty seconds
So that I thought I would surely
Pass out, but he finally let up.

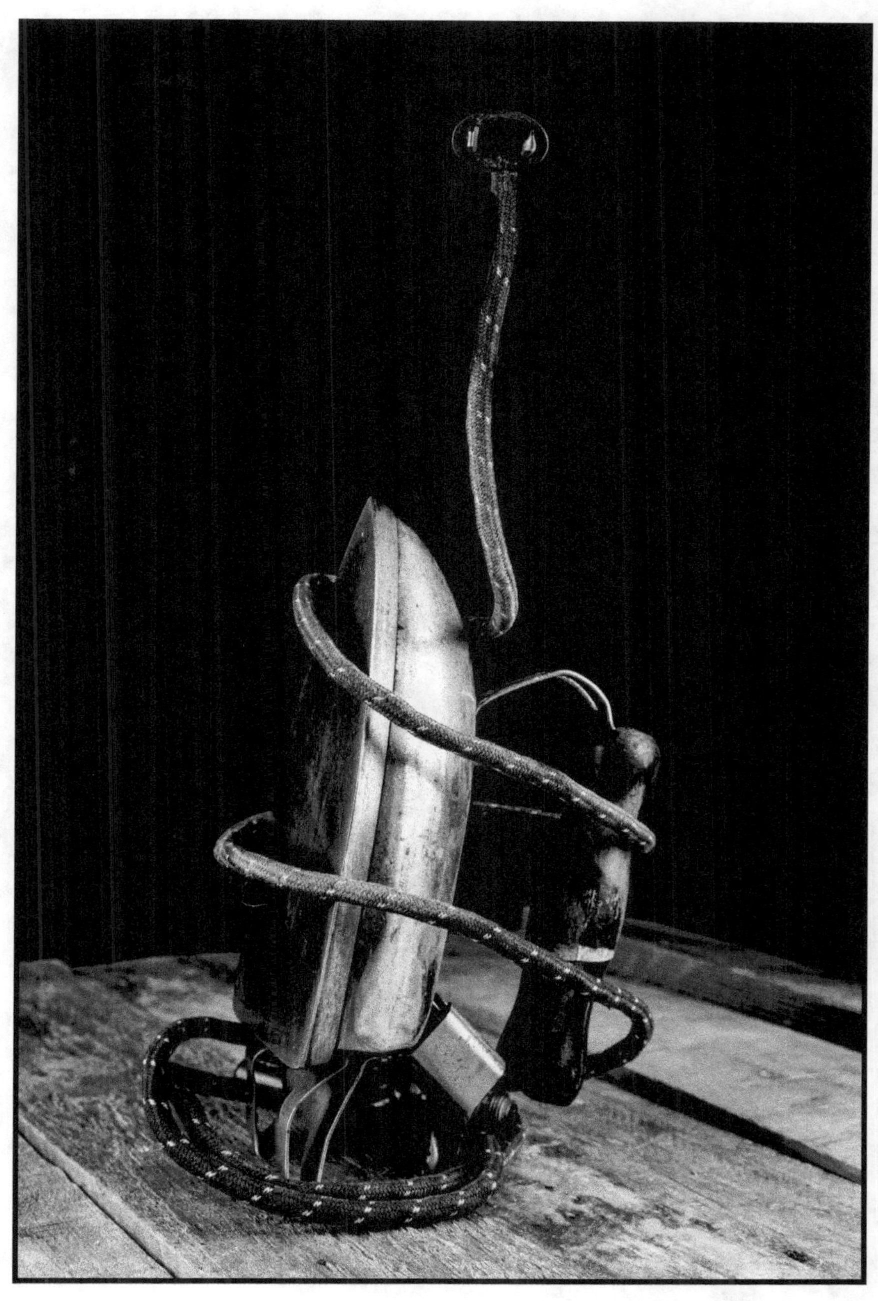

Then he said
I want to see who you got
On your facebook
And he sat there
In the other chair
Pushed up against me
Scrolling through
My list of 737 friends,
Unfriending anybody
He didn't know
Or who he thought
Had something
To do with the school.

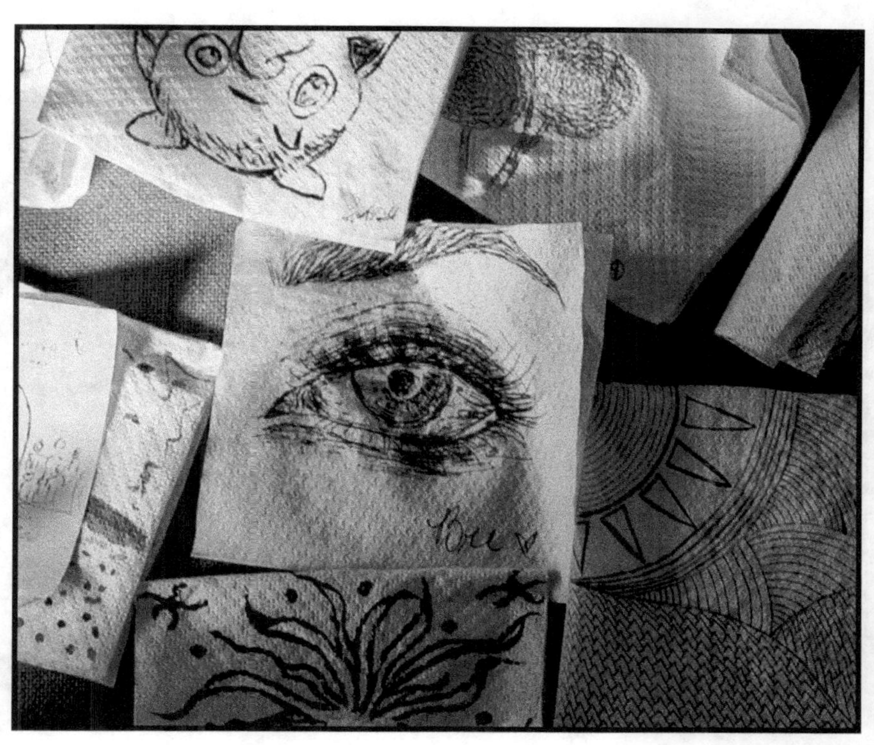

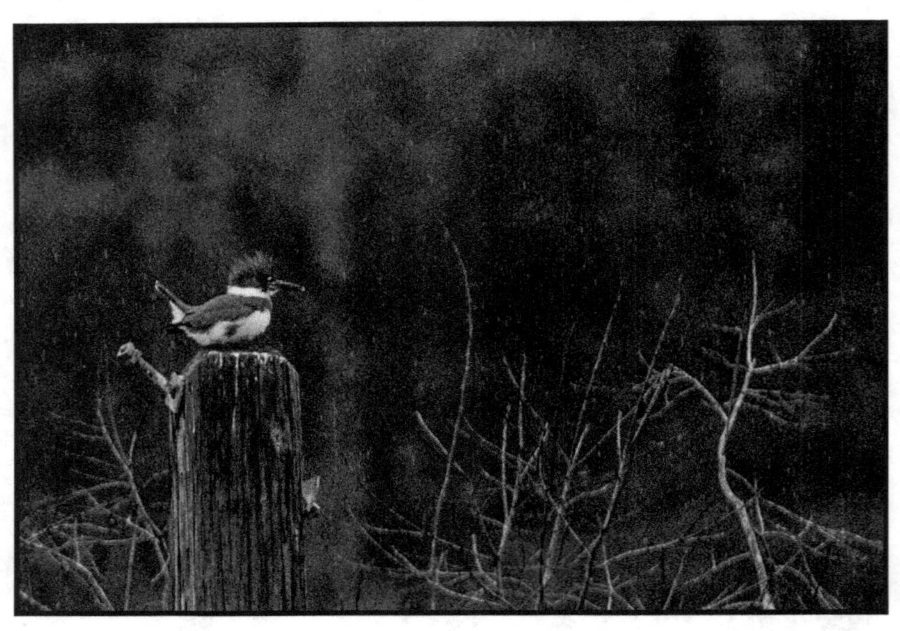

My throat felt like when
I had the strep winter a year ago,
But I didn't say anything.
I didn't cry like I had in the past
When he was cruel to me.
I sat there for an hour and a half
While he thinned my facebook
Down to less than 300 people.
At one point, he told me
To go get him a beer,
And I did.

In my early forties
I still have my figure,
And I can wear my jeans
Just like the young girls
In the program;
It kills Claude
To see some guy
Turn his head
To get a look at me,
But it happens all the time
And what am I supposed to do,
Put on grandma clothes
And hide in the kitchen.

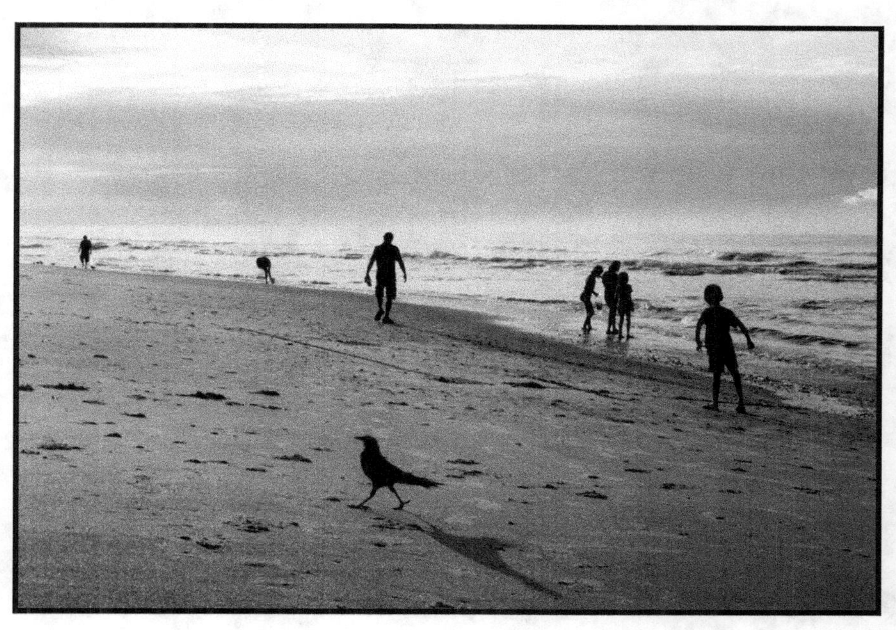

I can see him down
At the far end of the yard now
Making his turn and backup
To swing around the other way.
Snakeremoval.com
Says a copperhead
Can only strike a distance
Of one and a half
Times its length,
So he's still okay
For a couple more laps.

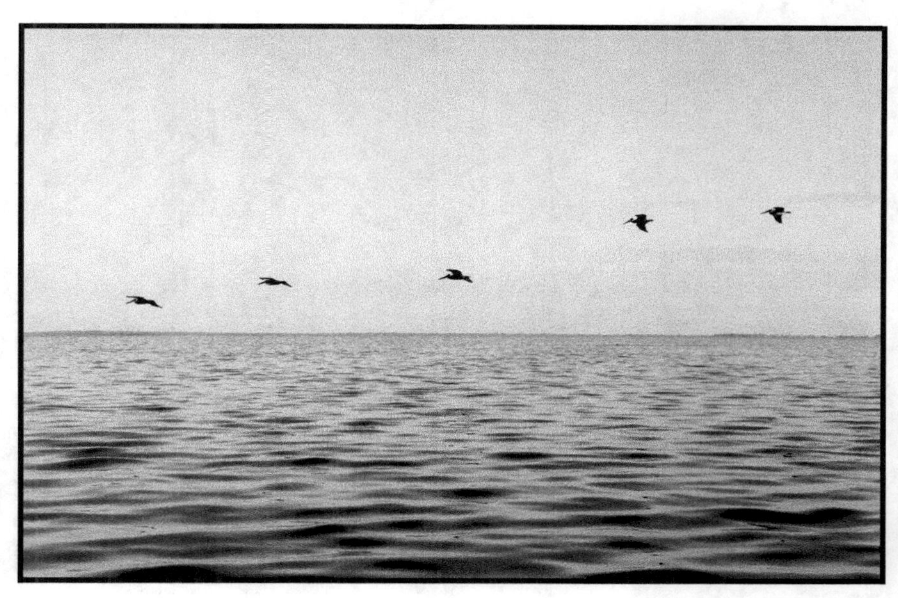

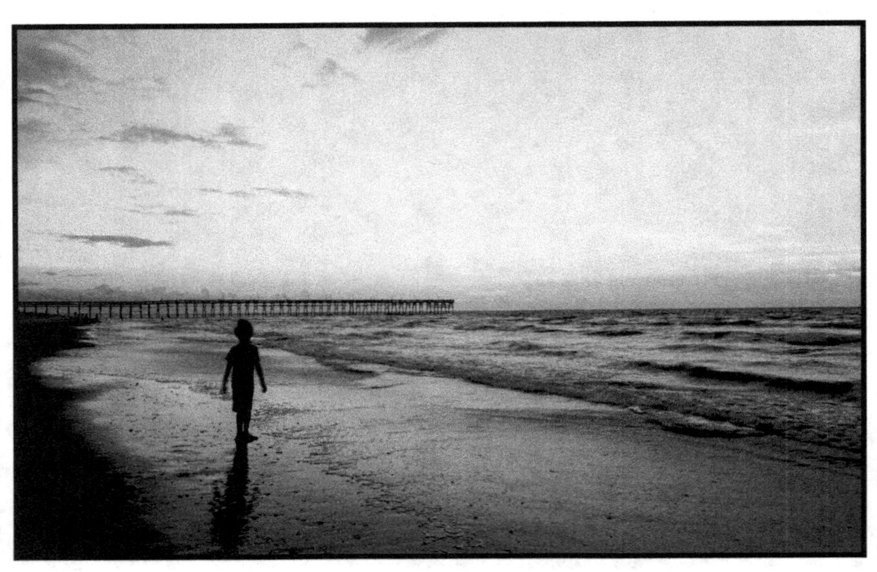

For years Claude wouldn't let me wear clothes to bed,
And sometimes I'd come out of a dream
And he'd be edging over on top of me;
I'm not complaining; I married a real man,
Big and tight muscled; he looked like
The guys on the baseball cards,
And that was the plan
Till he tore his shoulder
Ending the dream he'd had
Since he was a boy.

Now he pushes away from me,
Like there's a burning shame
Somewhere inside of him
For the shape he's gotten into,
For his boredom with his life,
His lack of feelings
For his own kids,
But mainly his ambivalence,
Another reading word,
Toward a wife
He no longer wants
But doesn't want
Anybody else to have.

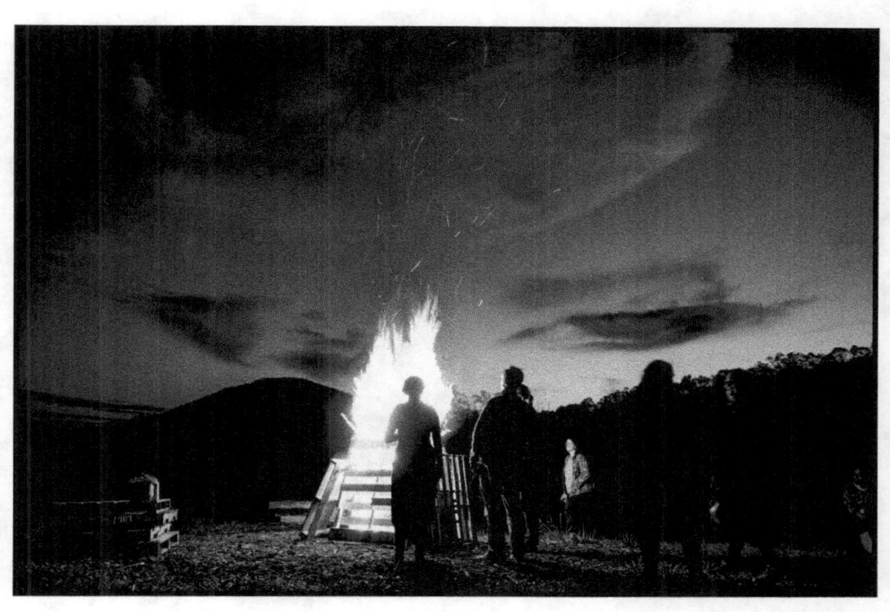

So there I said it,
How it is with us,
And I took the laptop
From the table
And put it in my lap,
Turning away
From the lawnmower
And the bird house
And the whole world out there.

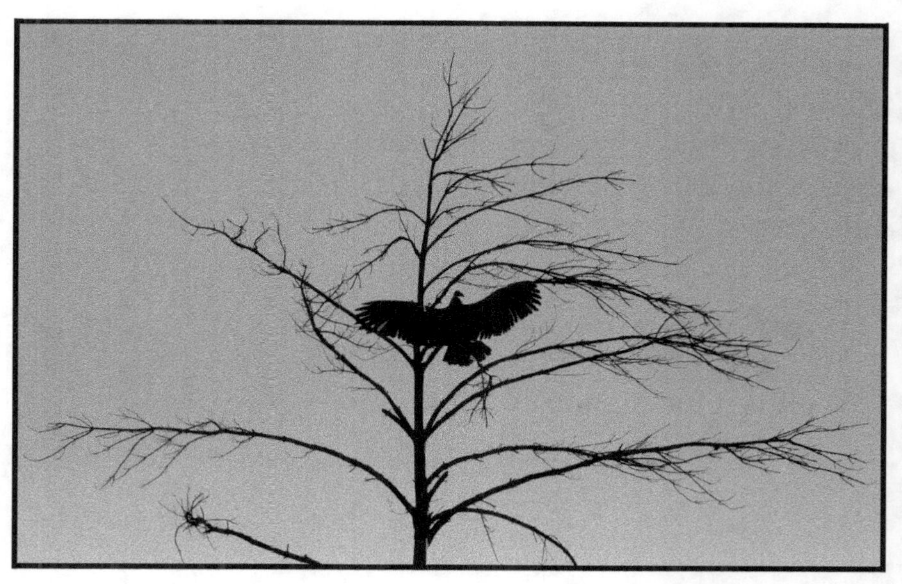

And I went to the school website
And clicked on Blackboard
For my Anatomy class,
About to study the vocabulary
For tomorrow's test
When the lawnmower shut down.
I couldn't turn to look.

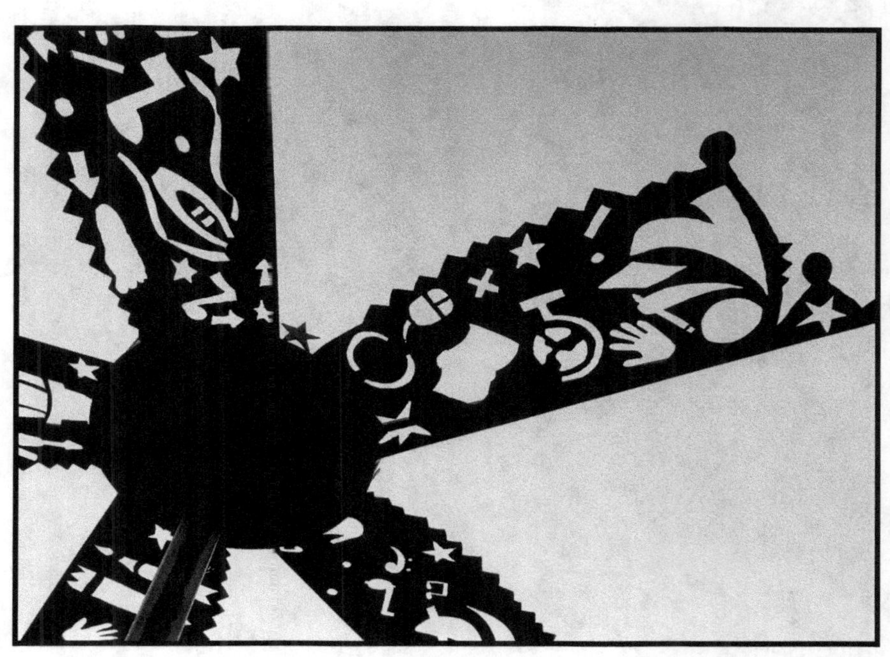

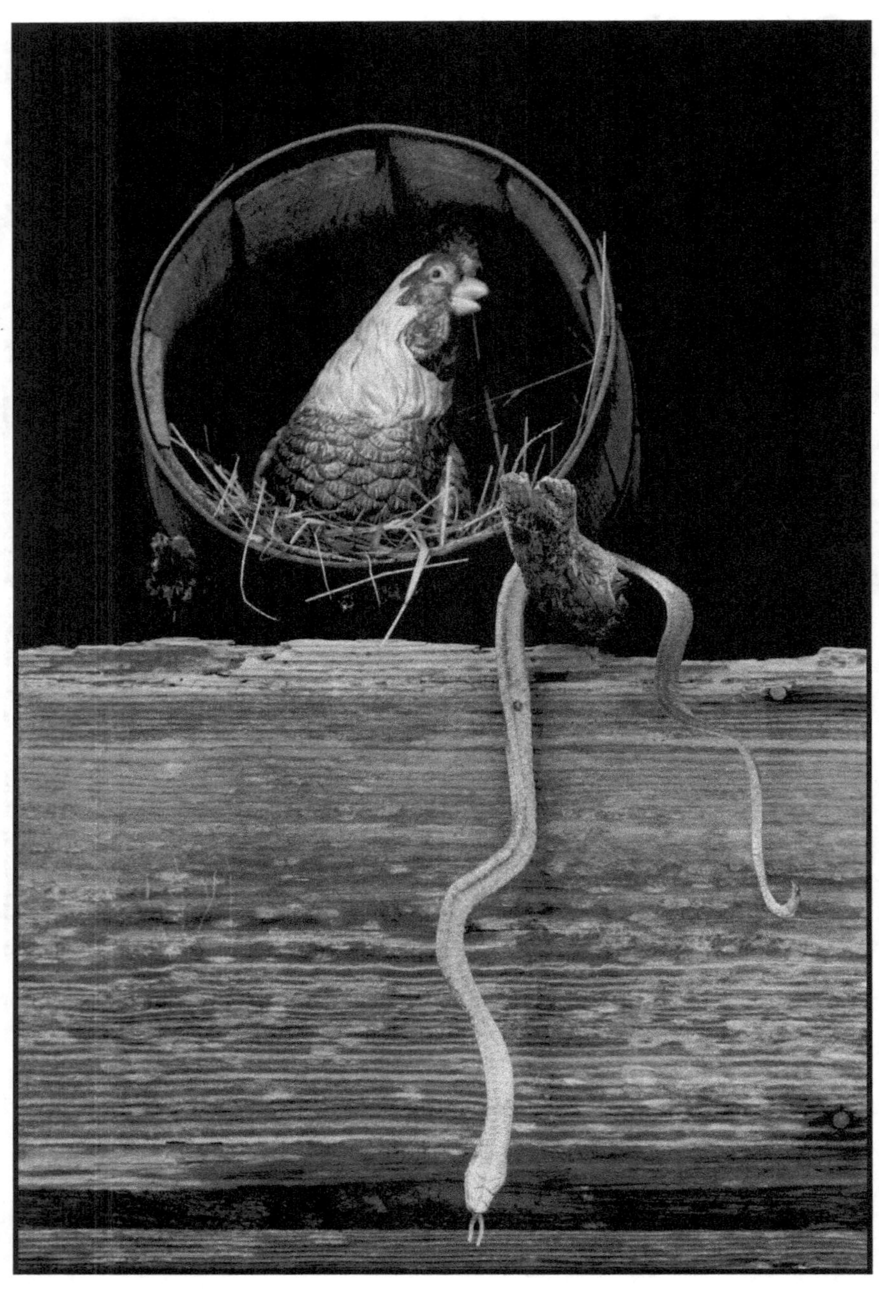

I knew the copperhead
Had gone for his neck,
And I imagined
The fat little devil,
Half-full of bird eggs,
Hanging there
Injecting all of its venom
As Claude jerked alert
From his lawn mowing stupor,
Unable to shake it loose.

The neighbor had told me
About his black lab a week ago,
How he'd let her go out to piss
Just after dark, and she
Went to the back of the yard
Into the high grass
He'd left for the last month,
How the copperhead struck her white belly
And she struggled to
The front of the house
Before she collapsed
In convulsions and died.

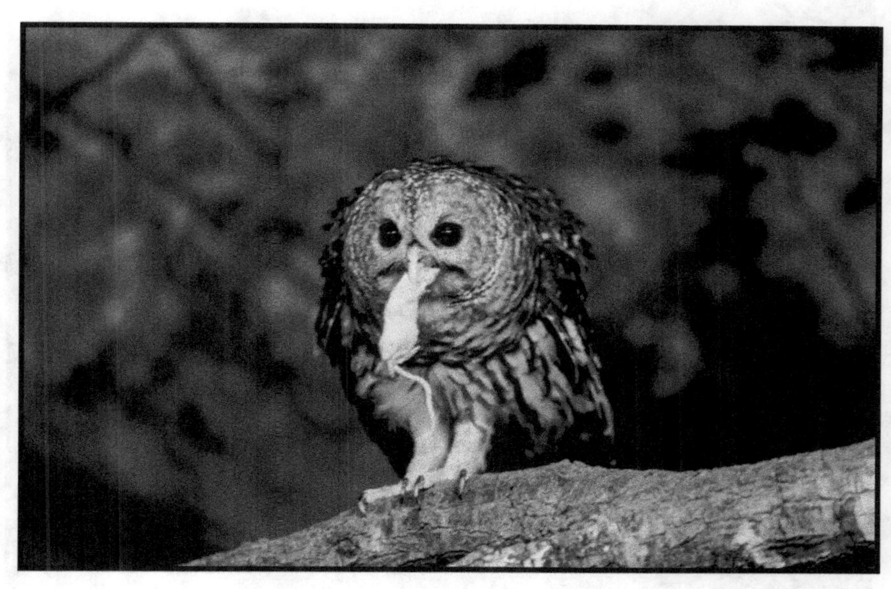

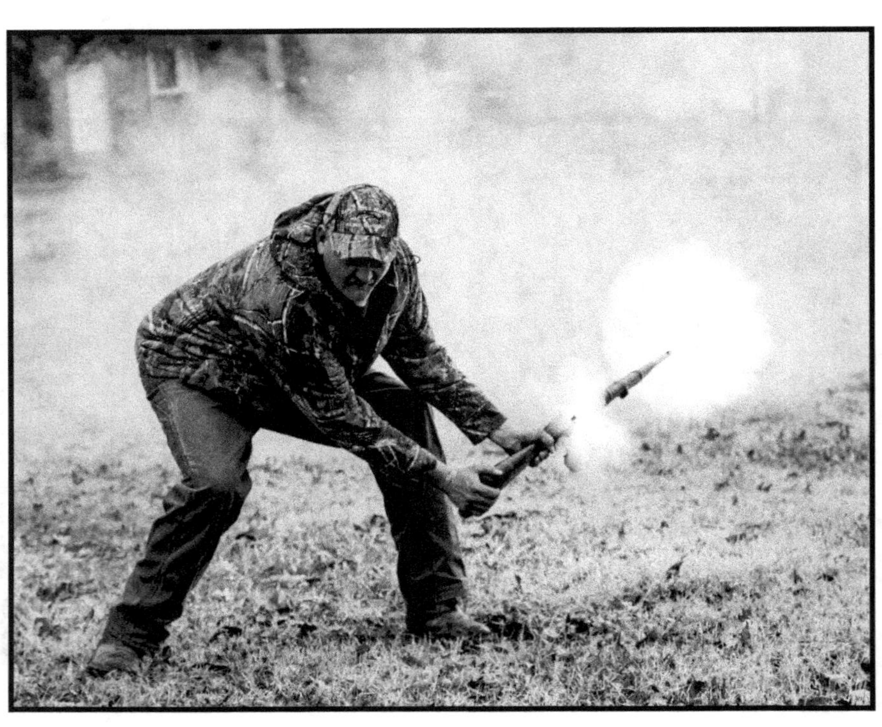

I waited to hear Claude
Yelling for help
But heard nothing
But the bare electrical hum
Of my laptop,
But I was still afraid
To turn around;
I didn't want to see
Claude lying in the yard
His face swollen
Like he'd been hit
By a gun shot.

Five minutes went by
But it seemed like an hour.
I was sick on my stomach
And I could barely focus
On this diagram
That showed and named
The different parts
Of the human heart.

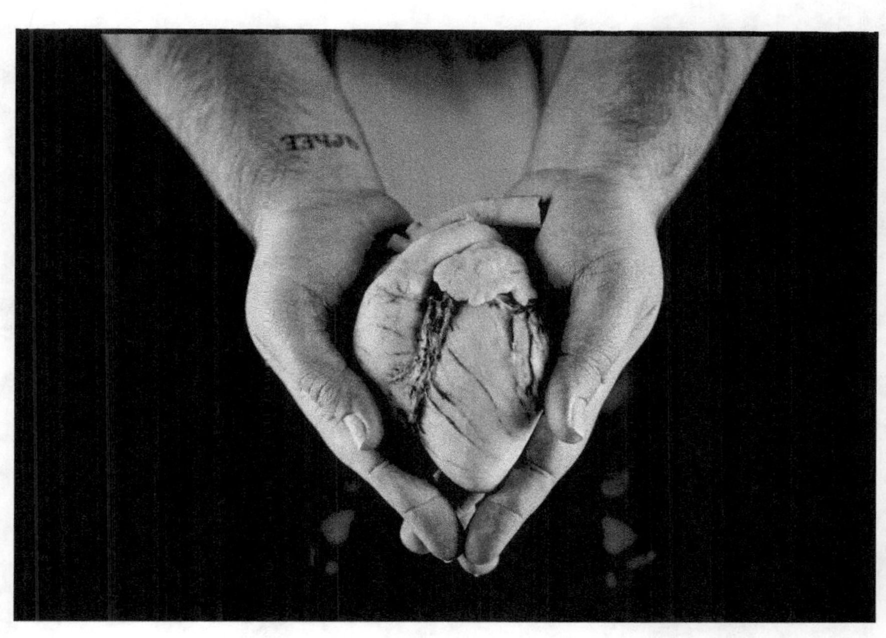

I clicked on the right side of the heart
And the terms lit up; as I was about
To click on the left side of the heart,
The porch door to the sun room
Suddenly swung open, a familiar
Hairy tattooed arm reached in,
Dropped the copperhead
On my polished wood floor
And slammed the door shut.

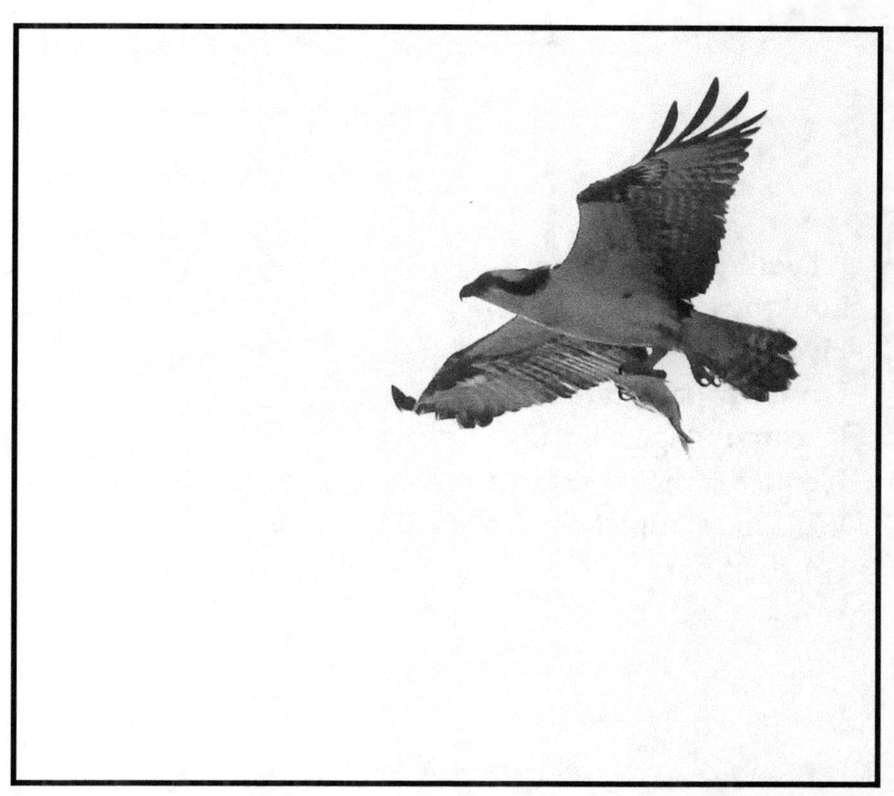

It lay there
Looking at me,
Five feet away
From my bare, tanned legs.
Its camouflage coloring
Blended almost perfectly
With the stain I'd chosen
For the floor.

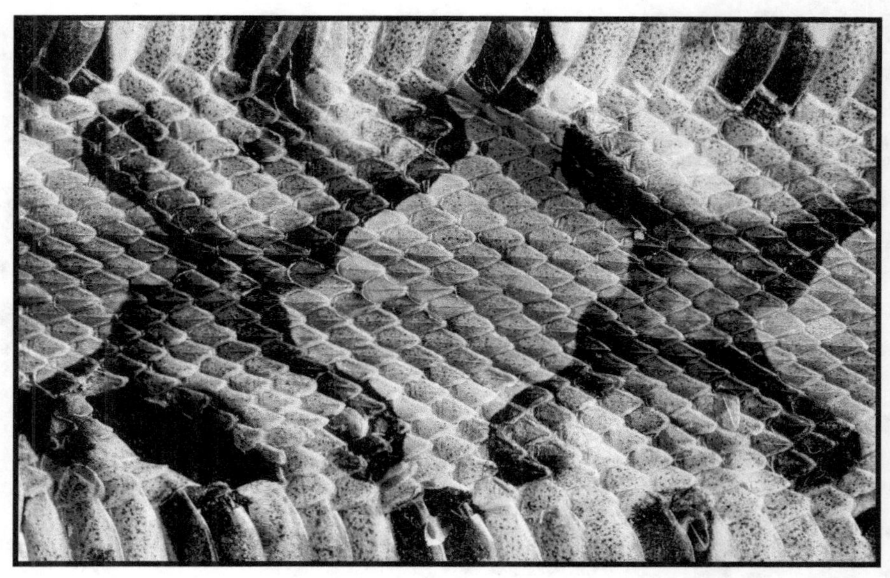

It watched me through its slit eyes,
Resting its shovel -shaped head
On a running shoe I'd kicked off earlier;
The snake was the second most coldblooded
Animal I'd ever seen this close,
And I knew as sure as I knew
That I was leaving Claude
When I finished the program
That I could sit here
Absolutely still,
Frozen in this moment of my life,
For however long it took.

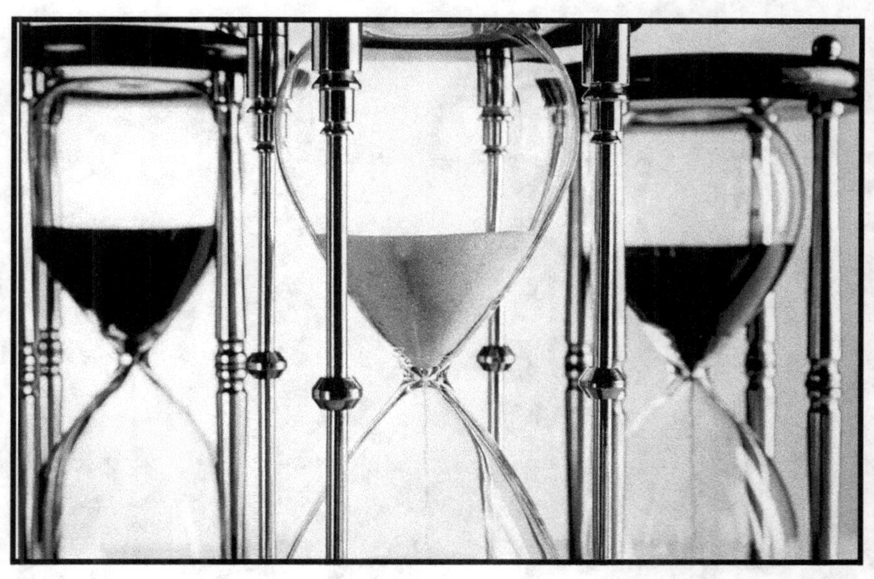

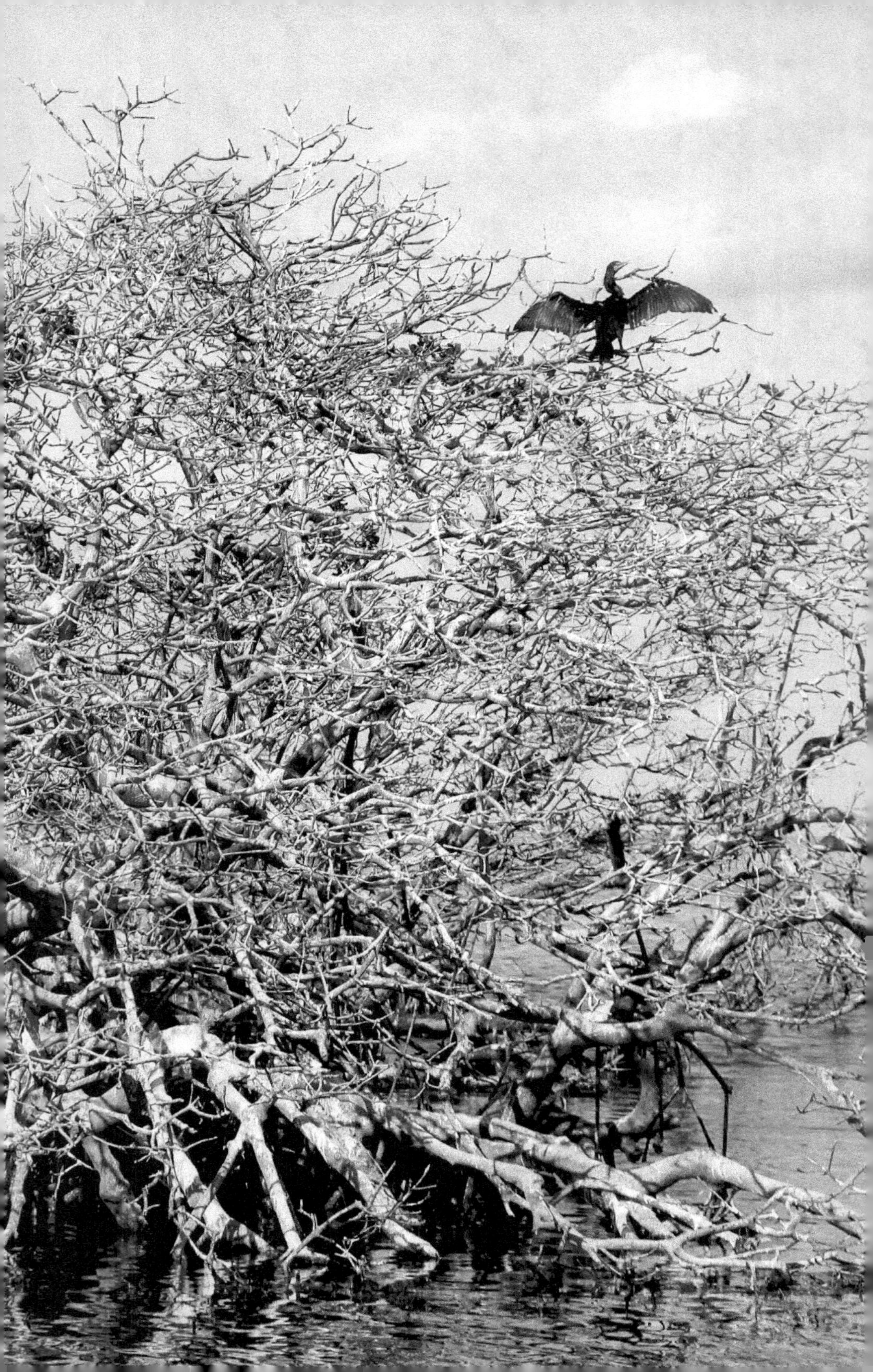

www.ingramcontent.com/pod-product-compliance
Lightning Source LLC
LaVergne TN
LVHW020049110826
845155LV00029B/699

9781952485039